ETIQUETTE

FERN G. BROWN ETIQUETTE

Illustrated by Anne Canevari Green

Franklin Watts
New York/London/Toronto/Sydney/1985
A First Book

SOUTH HUNTINGTON
PUBLIC LIBRARY
2 MELVILLE ROAD
HUNTINGTON STATION, N.Y. 11746

j
395
BRO

*For my mother, who
knows all the rules*

Library of Congress Cataloging in Publication Data

Brown, Fern G.
Etiquette.

(A First book)
Includes index.
Summary: Presents "new etiquette," which combines
consideration for others with new ideas of honesty and
sincerity, for use at home, at school, and in public.
1. Etiquette for children and youth. [1. Etiquette]
I. Green, Anne Canevari, ill. II. Title.
BJ1857.C5B65 1985   395'.122   84-20935
ISBN 0-531-04908-6

Copyright © 1985 by Fern G. Brown
Illustrations copyright © 1985 by Anne Canevari Green
All rights reserved
Printed in the United States of America
5 4 3 2 1

249030

CONTENTS

Introduction 1

Chapter One
When You Are at Home 5

Chapter Two
When You Are at School 32

Chapter Three
When You Are Out in Public 44

Chapter Four
When You Are at a Party 56

Chapter Five
When You Are Making Introductions 65

Chapter Six
When You Are a House Guest 68

Chapter Seven
When You Are Writing a Letter 74

Index 83

ACKNOWLEDGMENTS

The author and editors express their appreciation to the following individuals for their assistance in the preparation of this book:

Carol Mueller and Patricia Vyn, Director, Wilmot Elementary School Library Media Center, Deerfield, Illinois; Shirley Peterson, Parents Without Partners, Deerfield, Illinois; Richard Stern, Manager, Wilmette Theater, Wilmette, Illinois; Dennis Meritt, Assistant Director, and Louise Bower, Librarian, Lincoln Park Zoo, Chicago, Illinois; Bill Haberichter, Director, Oehler Funeral Home, Arlington Heights, Illinois; C. Wesley Barnett, D.D.S., Chicago, Illinois; employees of Deerfield, Illinois, Post Office; members of Des Plaines Valley Horsemen's Association of Illinois; Marsha Brown and Joanne Smith for nutrition and exercise information.

ETIQUETTE

INTRODUCTION

Don't let the word *etiquette* scare you. It simply means having good manners—treating others the way you want them to treat you.

Etiquette isn't something that your parents and teachers dreamed up. It's been around for thousands of years. Rules of good behavior have been handed down from one generation to the next through the centuries. The first book of manners was written on papyrus, before paper was invented.

During the seventeenth century, the nobles in the royal courts of France and England followed these long-established rules and also added some new ones. The word "etiquette" comes from French and German words meaning "to stick" or "to affix." Rules for daily conduct were posted or stuck to walls in palace courtyards. They were called *l'estiquets* or *l'estiquettes*, which meant "the tickets" or "the stickers." When the rules changed, new *estiquettes* were substituted. Later, they became books of etiquette.

When Europeans settled in the New World, they brought their notions of etiquette with them. (George Washington

kept a notebook of rules of conduct, adapted from a work of an earlier period.) Etiquette books began to appear, written by people who thought social behavior in the new country needed improvement. Many of the pioneers, though, didn't read the books; they lived simple lives and had their own rough rules of conduct. After all, there was no privileged upper class in America, and everyone was supposed to be socially equal. Why would they need etiquette books?

Gradually, as more people settled in the United States, social conduct became more complex. The Industrial Revolution brought about new inventions and new wealth. People needed an authority to tell them how to behave when using confusing new luxuries such as the telephone and the automobile. They welcomed some guidance in how to live in a world that was becoming more complicated and more struc-

— 2

tured. In 1922, when Emily Post wrote her famous book, *Etiquette, the Blue Book of Social Usage,* the majority of Americans were ready for it. Whenever they were in doubt as to what to do in a specific situation, they would ask, "What does Emily Post say?" and look for the answers in her book. Americans lived by Mrs. Post's book and similar books of formal etiquette for almost forty years.

In the sixties and seventies, the young people of America ignored the old rules of behavior and made their own. They didn't care what Emily Post and others had said. Old-fashioned etiquette was "out." Theirs was a new, "sincere" style of behavior, characterized by an unwillingness to conform to established conventions.

The traditional family structure and the roles of men and women are changing. In the past, women were thought to be the weaker sex, in need of protection, and men were

expected to behave with special politeness toward them. Modern women fought for equality with men in social, economic, and legal matters, and now society is much less rigid about rules concerning male-female relationships.

Etiquette is "in" again, but it's different. We have retained the basic idea of consideration for others and blended it with the new ideas of honesty and sincerity popular during the last twenty years.

How does the new etiquette affect you? People judge you by the way you act—when you are at home, at school, at the movies, at a party, making introductions, as a house guest, and even by the way you write a letter. As you move out into the world, you are going to confront new situations, have new experiences, and make new friends. This book will give you suggestions and guidelines for your conduct. If you have a question about manners, look it up. Rules of behavior may differ according to local customs and your family ceremonies and traditions. These aren't rigid rules, but they do tell you how to behave so you'll be comfortable in new situations and know what's expected of you.

The new etiquette may be more flexible than that of the past, but the basic idea is still the same—common sense and consideration for others.

1 WHEN YOU ARE AT HOME

You weren't born with manners. When you were a baby, if you wanted food or a toy, you reached out and took it. It didn't matter whether it belonged to you. You cried even if it was the middle of the night. You didn't care if you woke the whole neighborhood.

When you were old enough to understand, your parents began to teach you how to behave correctly. You learned to ask for things, not to grab; you learned to drink from a cup and to eat with a spoon and fork. You were taught to say "please" and "thank you." You were learning etiquette so you could live with others according to acknowledged rules of behavior.

Home is the best place to practice kindness, sharing, and consideration for others. You won't always be on your best behavior, but basic caring for others starts in your home.

YOUR PARENTS

Your parents have had more experience in living than you've had. Even if you don't agree with them, respect their opinions. Parents should also let you voice your opinions and listen when you talk. They should be your models for behavior.

With your parents' guidance and supervision, you will learn to make decisions, to be self-reliant, and to be independent.

What Do You Call Your Parents?
It's been a long-standing custom for children to call their parents by words derived from "mother" and "father." You probably call your mother "Mom" and your father "Dad." In the past, it was thought disrespectful to call a parent by his or her first name. But if your friend Jeff's mother approves of him calling her "Nancy," it's not bad manners, it's their choice.

It is perfectly acceptable to call a stepparent by his or her first name. How you address your parents should be decided in your home.

Getting Along with Your Parents

It's not always what you say, it's how you say it. If your mother tells you to take out the garbage and you say "okay," it seems as if you're cooperating. But are you? The tone of your voice can make "okay" a cheerful, I'll-do-it-willingly word or a disgusted, why-does-she-always-pick-on-me word.

If you use the disgusted tone, it will spoil the communication between you and your mother. If it's the cheerful one, she'll know you're cooperating and will do her best to be on good terms with you.

Treating Parents with Respect

Treat your parents with the same respect as you do other adults. Say hello when they come home from work. After all, you are one of the reasons they're working. Help your mother put on her coat; carry packages for her; and remember to hold the door open for your father and your mother. Answer when your parents talk to you. Say "Yes, Dad," or "No, Dad," instead of "Yah" and "Nope," which aren't really words.

Parents like compliments. Tell your mother how nice she looks in her new dress. Say you like your father's hairstyle. An honest compliment often helps make up for the difficult times.

Tell your parents when you're going out. Let them know that you're biking over to a friend's house to do homework—or going to the library. It's important so they won't worry about where you are or what you're doing. Let them know when you expect to return, too. If you trust them with your plans, they'll trust you.

When you have a problem, talk it out. Parents aren't mind readers. Unless you tell her, your mother won't know you're angry because she scheduled you for the dentist on the day of the soccer tryouts. Talking things over is the best way to work through problems, large or small.

Your Parents' Rules
Rules are important because they tell you what's expected of you. If there were no rules to live by in your home, you would think your parents didn't care about you or what you do. When your mother or father makes a rule, there is always a reason for it.

Don't nag your parents to change their minds once they've said no. Whining and nagging only makes matters worse. It's not disrespectful, however, to ask your parents to explain their decisions, and to give them some good solid reasons why you don't agree.

That old argument, "Everybody's doing it; why can't I?" won't work if you're talking about curfew or doing homework in front of the TV. Your parents have set their standards and probably won't change them. But if you tell them that all your sixth-grade classmates are wearing T-shirts and

jeans to school and they would think you were weird if you wore your best clothes, maybe your parents will allow you to wear what the others do. What you wear to school is a matter of what's in style, not of changing basic ideas and values that are important to your parents.

If Your Parents Are Divorced
If your parents are divorced, it's natural for you to feel a sense of loss for the parent you see less often. But you still have two parents. Treat both of them with respect, no matter which one you live with, and obey the rules of whichever home you are in.

Most divorced parents want to keep their children's lives as stable and regular as possible. The parent you live with will probably treat you the same way he or she always did. The parent you don't live with should not be expected to entertain you and buy you presents every time you see each other. Sometimes it's fun to take a quiet walk and have a confidential talk, or just to watch TV together or share other activities.

When you're denied something by your mother, don't say, "But Dad lets me." Or if your father tells you not to do something, don't say, "Why not? Mom says it's okay." If you're being punished, don't call your other parent to complain. You'll anger the one who is trying to teach you a sense of values.

It is bad manners to report back to one parent what is going on in the other parent's home. If your mother wants to know about your father's private life, don't talk about it. If your dad questions you about your mother's private life, say, "You'll have to ask Mom." You are entitled to privacy and so are your parents.

Sometimes it's easier to talk about your feelings to your stepmother or stepfather than to your own parents. A fairly impartial person who is willing to listen might help solve your problems.

Your Parents' Friends
Ask your parents' friends what they prefer to be called. It will probably be a first name like "Sue" or "Ed." If they are more formal, call them by their last name; for example, "Mister and Mrs. Aberman."

Practice your manners on your parents' friends. When the doorbell rings, don't lounge in front of the TV and pretend you're not there—walk to the door. If it's someone you know, smile and say, "Hello, Mrs. Shepard. How are you?" and put out your hand. It's a simple, friendly greeting. Or you might say, "Hi, Mrs. Shepard. Haven't seen you in a long time." If you're feeling super-friendly you might add, "How's Jennifer? Is she going to summer camp?" Invite Mrs. Shepard to come in and sit down. When she does, you may sit, too.

If your father has told you he's expecting someone you haven't met, answer the door and say, "Hello, Mister Krinn." Shake hands and introduce yourself. Then say, "Dad is expecting you. Please come in." Your good manners will make Mr. Krinn feel welcome.

YOUR FAMILY

It's the little things in life that make living together easier and more pleasant. Good manners are not just for special occasions. They should be an important part of your daily life.

*How to Get Along
Well with Your Family*

Say "Good morning" or "Hi" to each family member when you first see him or her each morning. Use the words "please" and "thank you" at home as much as possible. You probably say them automatically when you're out in public, but a simple "Thank you for the nice dinner, Mom" might surprise your mother and make her feel good.

Do your jobs willingly. Don't be the one who always runs out or pretends to do homework when you're supposed to be doing dishes. It's a good idea to rotate chores so you aren't stuck doing something you hate every night.

Whether it's a picnic or painting the garage, any project can be fun if your family does it together. Don't be a spoiler who ruins the fun for the rest of the family. Instead of saying "I hate doing it," enter into family projects with enthusiasm and everyone will have a good time.

If someone in your family receives special news, congratulate him on the good news and console him for the bad.

Suppose your sister won a good-sportsmanship trophy at school. Say, "Congratulations, Sis, that's great," and help her celebrate. If your older brother hears he didn't make the first team in football, console him with something like, "Plenty of guys wish they could play as well as you." It will help him deal with his disappointment.

Everyone makes mistakes. If you've made one, admit it. Say you're sorry. Then, if possible, correct your mistake, and try not to let it happen again. Your apology won't change what you did, but it tells the other person you're sorry, and that you care.

Your Brothers and Sisters

Because you live in the same home, you see a lot of your brothers and sisters. You may be close to all of them, or one brother or sister may be your special friend. Remember that each of you is an individual with a different personality and a different set of problems. You have to work at getting along together.

Try not to be jealous or envious of your brothers or sisters. They have the same right to share your parents' love and attention that you do.

Don't be a tattletale. When your sister has overstayed her curfew, that's her problem. Let her work it out with your parents. If you don't mind your own business, she may never want to be friends with you again.

Your Grandparents
If your grandmother lives with you or if she comes to visit, make her feel loved and needed. Treat her with kindness and respect, and she will give you love and respect in return. Whether your grandmother is the type who sews and bakes cookies or the kind that goes bowling and is active in the League of Women Voters, you can learn a great deal from her. Take the time to listen and let her in on what's happening in your life. A close relationship with an adult of another generation can make you more understanding of older people's problems.

If you have a grandparent in a nursing home, don't neglect him or her. It's lonely to be apart from your family. Write and telephone regularly, and visit as often as possible. When you visit, bring a gift. It doesn't have to be a big one— a new comb, some favorite candy, or a picture you've drawn will be fine. Allow enough time to have a conversation. He or she looks forward to your company.

Family Privacy
Although your family is a unit, everyone—including your parents and grandparents—has a right to privacy. If you respect others' privacy, they will respect yours.

Never read anyone else's letters without permission, or even peek at a diary that doesn't belong to you. Don't be a pest who listens in on private phone conversations. Treat every family member respectfully, even your youngest brother or sister.

If your brother's door is closed, knock before you enter. When your door is closed, your brothers and sisters will do the same. But don't overdo being a loner. If your door is always closed, the family will feel shut out of your life. And if you lock your door, they will think you don't trust them.

When you share a room with one or more of your brothers or sisters, you can't shut the door and keep them out when you want to be alone. Instead, decide with them on certain hours of the day or times during the week when you can each have the room to yourself. Rotate the hours to make it fair for everyone. You might also ask your parents' permission to use another room in the house or apartment if you need more privacy.

*Talking to Outsiders
about Your Family*
Don't complain to outsiders about your family. If you do, it will reflect on you because you are part of that family. Talk over your complaints at home.

If your mother says not to tell that she is going to change jobs, keep it a family secret. Don't tell anyone—not even your best friend. If you do, you may get your mother into trouble with her present boss. Family secrets should stay in the family.

YOUR RESPONSIBILITIES

Whether you share a room or have one of your own, it probably costs your parents a lot of time, money, and effort to give you this privilege. Show them you appreciate it by keeping your room reasonably clean and neat.

Keeping Your Room Neat
Make your bed before you leave in the morning. When the bed is made, the whole room looks neat. Put your pajamas away. Throw your dirty clothes in the laundry hamper instead of letting them pile up on a chair. You may want to

sit on the chair to do your homework. Hang up clean clothing so you can wear them again. Fold sweaters and put them into drawers; they stretch out of shape if you hang them up. It only takes a few minutes each day to keep your room looking neat.

Keeping the House Clean
Clean up after yourself when you have a snack. Wash your drinking glasses or put them in the dishwasher. Don't leave dirty dishes around. Nobody should have to clean up after you.

Finished playing? Pick up all games, cards, and toys and put them in their proper places. The next time you or someone else wants to use them, you won't have to search the drawers and closets.

The TV
You don't have to depend on TV for all your entertainment. You can have fun by discovering the outdoors, taking part in sports, reading, playing games, and having hobbies and collections.

But you can also reap the benefits of TV if you don't let it control you. Your parents should make firm rules for TV viewing. A strict time limit, with parental approval of programs, will work if you stick to it.

Some families have made it a rule not to turn on the TV during the week. Others have set the daily limit for TV viewing at one or two hours. Whatever your parents' rules are, with a time limit for viewing, you'll probably choose your programs more carefully.

Other important rules are (1) don't do homework in front of the TV; (2) don't talk about TV programs at the dinner

table to the exclusion of other topics; (3) don't play the TV too loud, especially when others are trying to sleep; and (4) turn off the TV when you leave the room.

The Bathroom
If you share a bathroom, your parents should make rules about when and how long each person can use it. If you and your sister leave for school at the same time, perhaps you can make your bed while she uses the bathroom. She will make her bed later while you take your turn in the bathroom.

Everyone should have his or her own towel, washcloth, drinking glass, and oral hygiene materials and a place to keep them. This is necessary to prevent the spread of germs that cause disease.

When you're finished in the bathroom, hang up wet towels. Pick up your dirty clothes from the floor and re-cap the toothpaste. Check for spills and hair in the washbasin and wipe it clean. Mop up puddles on the floor so the next person doesn't slip and fall. Wash the dirt off the soap and wipe out the soap dish. Clean the bathtub or shower if it needs it. If the mirror over the basin is steamed up, wipe it off. Hang the bath mat over the tub to dry, and spread the shower curtain wide. Boys, leave the toilet seat down.

If the soap, toilet paper, or shampoo has run out, the last person to use it should go to the cupboard or closet wherever it is kept, and replace it.

Your Allowance
The purpose of having an allowance is to learn to manage and handle money. The amount of your allowance depends on what your parents consider appropriate and what it is expected to cover.

It is a good idea for you to earn a weekly allowance by doing household chores. Your parents will set the amount. If you do extra work, you'll get more. But you shouldn't expect to get paid for everything you do around the house.

Make saving a habit by putting aside a certain amount of your allowance every week. Keep a record of what you save, earn, and spend. Then open a bank account and watch your money grow.

Borrowing
Never borrow without permission. When you do borrow, even if it's your little brother's yo-yo, take better care of it than you would if it were yours. In the event that it gets

accidentally lost or broken, replace or repair it as soon as possible.

TABLE MANNERS

Practice your table manners at home and they will become automatic so you won't ever have to worry about how you look when you eat.

Some Simple Rules
You have probably been told many times to sit up at the table. That's good advice, but don't sit so stiffly that your back aches. When you're not eating, keep your hands in your lap or rest your forearms on the table. It's perfectly proper to rest your elbows on the edge of the table between courses.

When you're eating, keep your elbows close to your body so you won't bump the person next to you. Rest your other hand on the table next to your plate. It's easier than placing it in your lap. But don't keep your free elbow on the table; it's not only sloppy posture but it makes it difficult for the person next to you to carry on a conversation.

Don't touch your head at the table; a hair might fall in the food. Use the silverware for eating; don't play with it or scrape it against your plate.

When you bring food to your mouth, don't bend halfway toward the plate to meet it. And don't make noises or smack your lips. It's all right to talk during meals, but only when there is little or no food in your mouth. If you talk with your mouth full, it's not very appetizing for those around you, and nobody will understand you anyway.

You may take the pepper if it's close by, but don't reach across anyone or stand up and knock over a glass to get it. All you have to say is, "Please pass the pepper," and the person nearest to the pepper will pass it. If you are asked to pass something in a serving dish, such as bread, don't pick up one piece and pass it; always pass the entire serving dish.

Setting the Table
One way to learn about where to place forks, spoons, and knives is to help set the table. No matter what kind of dishes or silverware your family uses, the table is set the same way. The fork goes to the left of the plate. The folded napkin usually goes to the left of the fork, but it can also be placed on the plate. Place the knife to the right of the plate, with the cutting edge toward the plate. Put the spoon on the right of the knife. The drinking glass is placed above the knife.

The Napkin
If a prayer before eating is said in your home, don't pick up your napkin until it's over. Then unfold the napkin and put it in your lap. Use the napkin to wipe your mouth when you eat or drink. If you're served finger food, don't lick your fingers, use your napkin. When you finish your meal, place your napkin loosely gathered next to your plate. If you have to leave the table during a meal ask, "May I be excused?" Then put your napkin on your chair; it's usually too messy to leave on the table. When you come back, put it in your lap once more.

The Fork
Most food is eaten with a fork. Soft foods may be cut with a fork instead of a knife. In the American style of eating, we put the fork in the left hand to hold something for cutting. After it is cut, we put the fork in the right hand for eating.

(Left-handers usually hold the knife in the left hand for cutting, with the fork in the right hand. After the food is cut, the fork is shifted to the left hand for eating.)

Europeans avoid this constant switching of eating utensils by holding the knife with the right hand and the fork with the left, whether cutting the food or eating it.

The Knife
The knife is used for cutting. Hold the knife in the right hand. It is never held in the left hand unless you are left-handed. Cut one piece of food at a time and place the knife on the upper right-hand edge of the plate with the handle to the right, the blade on the plate.

When you finish eating, put your knife and fork side by side on the plate with their handles toward the bottom of the plate. The knife goes outside the fork with its cutting edge toward the center of the plate.

The Spoon
No matter what size it is, hold the spoon in your right hand (unless you are left-handed). There are some special rules for using a soup spoon. Only the side is put to your lips, then it's tipped a little so the liquid flows into your mouth. Never put the whole spoon into your mouth. When you get to the bottom of the soup bowl, you may tip the bowl away from you and use your spoon to eat the solid food. The spoon may be tipped either toward you or away from you to eat the last few spoonfuls. Rest your spoon on the plate under the bowl when you're finished. If the plate is too small, put the spoon in the bowl.

The same rule applies when you are finished stirring hot

chocolate. Place your teaspoon on the saucer, not in your cup or on the table.

A long-handled spoon may be left in a tall glass of, say, ice-cream parfait when there is no saucer.

*Sneezing and Blowing Your
Nose at the Table*
Leave the table if you have to blow your nose. If you can't help yourself, turn your head to one side and do it quickly and quietly. When you sneeze, hold your handkerchief or tissue—or at least your hand—in front of your nose and mouth to keep the germs from traveling to others. Don't use your napkin as a handkerchief.

Second Helpings
When your mother asks "Do you want a second helping of macaroni and cheese?" if you do, say "Yes, please." If you don't, say "No, thank you."

Eating Familiar Foods
It's perfectly all right to eat certain foods with your fingers. Here are some popular finger foods.

SANDWICHES: Cut sandwiches in half before eating them.

PIZZA: Hold your thumb on the bottom, two fingers around the edge; bend the wedge so the point goes up toward your mouth.

FRIED SHRIMP: Hold the shrimp by the tail and bite off a mouthful at a time. Place the tail on the side of your plate.

BARBECUED SPARERIBS: Cut one rib, pick it up and eat it. Then cut another. Ask for a separate plate for discarded bones.

OLIVES: Take a few bites to eat an olive. Put the pit on your salad or bread-and-butter plate. If you don't have one, use your dinner plate.

Sometimes you eat certain foods with a knife and fork and sometimes you eat them with your fingers.

FRIED CHICKEN: When served fried chicken with a knife and fork, put your fork in your left hand, and steady the piece of chicken. Cut it with your right hand, a bite at a time. (Left-handers reverse the process.) If you're at a picnic, you can eat the chicken with your fingers.

FRENCH-FRIED POTATOES: If you eat french fries with a meal, cut them into pieces and eat them with a fork. But if you are eating them with other finger food, such as hamburgers, you may eat them with your fingers.

Some foods you should never eat with your fingers. Spaghetti is one.

SPAGHETTI: Twirl the spaghetti around your fork and then carefully lift the fork to your mouth. If you can't manage this, you should cut the spaghetti with your fork.

BAKED POTATOES: Use a fork to butter or mash the potato. When you've finished eating the inside, it's healthy to eat the skin.

This is the way to eat fruits and vegetables when served at the table.
ASPARAGUS: Slender asparagus can be picked up and eaten with the fingers. Longer, thicker asparagus is eaten with a knife and fork. Cut off the tip and eat down the stalk, cutting one bite at a time. Leave the tough part of the stalk on the plate.
APPLES AND PEARS: When eating these fruits at the table, cut them into quarters and take out the seeds and core. You may also peel them if you wish. Then cut into small pieces and eat with your fingers.
GRAPES: Cut or break off a small cluster from the bunch of grapes and put it on your plate. Put one grape into your mouth at a time. If the grape has seeds, drop the seeds into your hand and put them on your dish.
BANANAS: Peel the banana and put the peel aside on your plate. Then break or cut off a piece of banana and eat it with your fingers.
GRAPEFRUIT: Grapefruit is eaten with a pointed teaspoon or an ordinary teaspoon. Take the seeds out of your mouth with the spoon. Never pick up the outer shell to squeeze out the last drop of juice—no matter how good it is.
ORANGES: Perhaps you can peel an orange in a continuous spiral, but an easier way is to section the skin with a knife and peel it off with your fingers. Then break the orange into parts and eat a section at a time. If you find seeds, put them in your hand and then on the side of your plate.
LEMONS: If it is a lemon wedge, pick it up, squeeze it

against your fork, and the juice will come out. If it's a slice, just press it with your fork on the plate.

MELONS: You may eat a section of cantaloupe with a dessert spoon or a knife and fork. Melon balls are eaten with a spoon. Watermelon served with the rind, the thick outer coat, is usually held in the hands. You may also lay a slice on its side, remove the pits with your fork, and cut bite-size pieces.

STRAWBERRIES: Fresh strawberries can be picked up by the stem and eaten with the fingers. If the berries are served with cream, in juice, or were frozen, eat them with a spoon.

STEWED FRUIT: When eating stewed plums or prunes, put pits onto your spoon and then onto the plate under your dish.

If you are in doubt as to how to eat something that you are served, watch your parents or others who seem to know what they are doing.

Taking Food Out of Your Mouth
You can use your thumb and forefinger to remove a bone or bit of food from your mouth—but don't call attention to it. Don't spit out food you don't like. If you eat soup that is too hot, take a sip of water to put out the fire. If there is something that is spoiled, like milk turned sour, it's all right to spit it out as quietly as possible.

TELEPHONE MANNERS

The telephone is a wonderful instrument, but it can cause many family disagreements. A few simple rules agreed upon by you and your parents will make your home life happier.

Here are some suggestions: (1) limit your phone calls to about five minutes; (2) tell your friends not to call at dinnertime or after nine o'clock in the evening; and (3) your friends should not call before breakfast, especially on weekends when your parents may want to sleep late.

When You Make a Call
If you aren't sure of a number, look it up in the telephone book first. If you can't find it, dial Information. Spell the last name; give the first name and, if possible, the address of the person whose number you want.

When you think you've dialed a wrong number ask, "Is this 945-4005?" If it's not, say, "I'm sorry. I have the wrong number," and hang up. Dial carefully this time. Allow at least six rings before hanging up. Your friend Ann may be practicing the piano or feeding the fish, and it's annoying for her to have to drop what she's doing and come to the phone only to find that you've hung up.

When someone says "Hello," reply clearly in a cheerful voice. Since we don't have phone-vision in our homes yet, the other party can't see you, and the tone of your voice is important. It's polite to say, "Hello, is Ann there?" and identify yourself. If Ann answers, just say "Hi," and begin the conversation. If Ann isn't there, leave your name and the time you'll call again, or ask that she call you. With a good friend like Ann, you don't have to leave your number. But if you call someone who is only an acquaintance, leave your number.

Many homes as well as businesses have telephone answering machines. When you call and find your friend's mother's answering machine is on, don't hang up. Leave a

— 25

simple message after you hear the musical tone or beep. "Hello, David. This is Blaine. Call me tonight before nine. I have something important to tell you." If David doesn't know your number, leave it on the machine.

When You Answer the Telephone
Answer the phone with a friendly "Hello." If the call is for you, say, "Yes, this is Marni." If the call is for your mother, "Just a minute, please, I'll call her" is the polite response. Don't bang the phone down and yell "Mom! Telephone!" Suppose your mother is putting the finishing touches on the chair she's varnishing. Go back to the telephone and say, "Please wait, she'll be here in a minute." Don't leave the caller hanging on the phone wondering if your mother got the message.

When the call is for someone who isn't home, say, "My sister isn't at home; may I take a message?" Then write it down. That's the only way you'll be sure to get the message right. Say "Please spell your name" if you're not sure of the spelling.

If you're home alone after school and the telephone rings, don't give out information about when the adults are returning unless you know who the caller is. Take the name and the message, and say "I'll ask Dad to call you when he comes in." This indicates the adults will be home soon.

When You Say Good-bye
Between friends, it doesn't matter who says good-bye first. You just say, "I have to go now, Ann, my mother wants the phone" or "Well, I've got to wash my hair now."

If it's a call between acquaintances, the one who makes the call is supposed to say good-bye first.

YOUR APPEARANCE

When people meet you for the first time, they don't know that you are a math whiz, a fantastic speller, and an all-around lovable person. They judge you by the way you look, stand, smell, and dress. So it pays to look your best. If you learn good grooming habits now, they will be a part of you for your entire life.

Eat a balanced diet daily, including four servings of fruits or vegetables, four servings of breads or cereals, three servings of milk or other dairy products, and two servings of meat, fish, eggs, or nuts. Drink six glasses of water daily, and get plenty of fresh air and exercise. Stay away from fried foods, too many fats, and gooey desserts. If you must eat sugar, eat it only with your meals. With this regime you'll stay in shape and keep from getting cavities.

Your Teeth Are Important
For good dental health, brush your teeth after meals and floss thoroughly at least once a day. Never lend anyone your toothbrush or borrow theirs.

BRUSHING. Use a fine-bristle soft toothbrush. Place the head of the toothbrush beside your teeth with the bristles angled against the gumline. Use a short, gentle, back-and-forth circular motion to clean the outer and inner surfaces of all your teeth. Then brush the chewing surfaces. Easy does it. Brushing too hard won't whiten your teeth, it will only remove the enamel. For the freshest-smelling breath, brush your tongue also.

FLOSSING. A toothbrush can't reach between your teeth, so use dental floss for your in-between toothbrush. Break off a long strand of unwaxed floss. Wrap some around one of your middle fingers and wrap the rest around the same finger on your other hand. Use your two thumbs, thumb and forefinger, or two forefingers to guide the floss between your teeth. Keep about an inch of floss between your fingers.

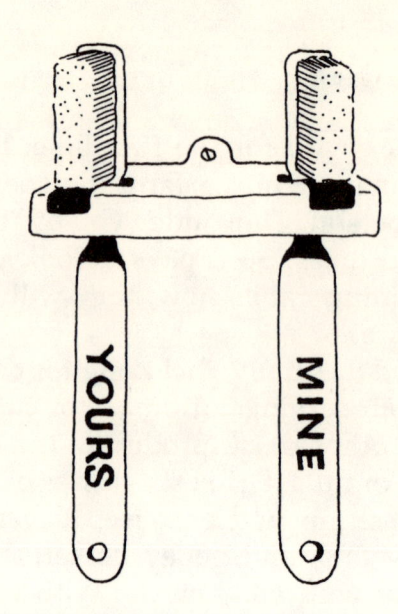

Use a gentle, sawing motion to insert the floss between your teeth. Don't snap the floss into your gums. When the floss reaches the gumline, push it against the back tooth and slide it away from the gum, scraping the tooth. Then pull the floss forward against the front tooth and repeat. After brushing and flossing your teeth, rinse your mouth.

Get regular dental check-ups. Be on time for your appointments, or come early. Take a book along in case you have to wait. Brush your teeth before you come.

Hair
Wash your hair once or twice a week. Use a shampoo that lathers well, and rinse thoroughly to get all the suds out.

While your hair is wet, comb through the tangles with a clean comb. Don't borrow anyone else's comb.

These days both boys and girls use hair dryers. If you do, follow directions and be sure to unplug the cord and put your dryer away afterwards.

Brushing is good for your scalp. It keeps your hair clean and shiny. But don't comb or brush your hair anywhere except in a bathroom or bedroom.

Hair style is a matter of what looks best on you. For girls, shiny, clean hair and a simple style are usually the best-looking. Boys should have their hair trimmed by a barber every six to eight weeks—whenever it gets too long.

Hands and Nails
Always wash your hands before eating and after going to the bathroom. Hand cream keeps hands soft, especially in winter when they tend to get rough and chapped.

Keep your fingernails clean by scrubbing them daily with soap and a nail brush. Never bite your fingernails. Learn to use a nail clipper. Boys, clip your fingernails and toenails straight across and short. Girls, clipping straight across is all right for toenails, but cut your fingernails to a medium length and file them into an oval shape with an emery board.

How You Sit and Stand
Don't slump! Stand with your back straight, shoulders back, and head erect. If you're tall, don't walk hunched over. If you're shorter than your friends, stand up straight—it will make you look taller.

When you sit, don't slouch or sit on the edge of your chair. Keep your back straight, feet flat on the floor, and your hands relaxed in your lap or on the arms of the chair.

How You Smell
How you smell depends on how clean and fresh you keep yourself. Wear clean underwear and socks every day. Take a daily bath or shower. If you ride your bicycle to school or take gym or after-school sports, you'll work up a sweat that no amount of cologne or talcum powder can cover. Remember, nothing takes the place of soap and water.

What You Wear
When you choose your clothes, follow the customs of your school or community. But wear styles and colors that look well on you. Ask yourself "How do I look in it?" and "Is it all right to wear it where I'm going?" The clothes you bought for your cousin Jeanette's wedding wouldn't be suitable for an evening at an amusement park. A pair of old jeans that are perfect for an amusement park would be wrong for a formal wedding.

Look at yourself in the mirror before you leave the house. Do your clothes fit? Are they clean? Yesterday's T-shirt will look and smell terrible, especially if it was lying crumpled on a chair all night. If it's dirty, don't wear it. Dirty clothes make a bad impression.

Perhaps your clothes are clean, but at the last minute you notice there is a button missing on your shirt. You run and get a safety pin, but your mother tells you the safety pin ruins your appearance. You put the shirt in the sewing basket and change shirts. You promise yourself that before you go to bed, you'll decide what you're going to wear tomorrow and look it over to be sure it's clean and that all the buttons are on. While you're checking your clothes, look over your shoes. Are they polished? Do they need heels? Are the shoelaces in good condition?

MORE MANNERS TO PRACTICE AT HOME

Learn how to accept a compliment. If your Aunt Ruth tells you she likes your jacket, don't say, "Oh, this old thing—I've had it for ages." You'll hurt her feelings and make her think she doesn't know what's in style. Instead, a simple "Thank you, Aunt Ruth" is the proper answer.

When your father is telling about his fishing trip, try to look interested. It's impolite to yawn in his face. If you must yawn, cover your mouth with your hand.

It's not good manners to belch in the presence of others. But if you can't keep it back, say "Excuse me."

Scratching your scalp, twirling a piece of hair, or cracking your gum is annoying to others even if you're concentrating on doing your homework and don't know you've offended anyone.

If you must chew gum, chew quietly with your mouth closed. When you're finished chewing, don't spit the gum on the floor. It's almost impossible to get gum off your shoe if you should step on it. Wrap the gum in paper and throw it into a waste container.

Don't swear. Using bad language doesn't make you big and smart. Swearing is a trick to see if you can shock your parents and friends and make them pay attention to you. There are other more constructive ways to get attention. Swearing can make you feel ridiculous and ashamed.

The manners you learn at home will make living with your family easier. And the more you use your manners the more they become a part of you.

2 WHEN YOU ARE AT SCHOOL

Bring the manners you've learned at home to school with you. At school you'll learn more rules of behavior. When you know what's expected of you, school will be a happy experience.

BUS MANNERS

Riding the bus is part of being in school. It's important to use your best manners on the school bus. If you distract the driver you could cause an accident.

Waiting at the Bus Stop
Get to the bus stop on time. Keeping twenty classmates waiting while you are a block away yelling for the driver to hold the bus is not being considerate of others.

Promptness is important, but don't arrive at the bus stop half an hour early either. Having nothing to do can get you into shoving matches and fights. Stand where you're supposed to, and don't play in the street or destroy your neighbor's landscaping.

When the bus comes, wait until it stops, then line up. Don't push to be the first one on. The bus won't leave without you.

How to Behave on the Bus
Choose a seat quickly, and remain seated for the entire ride. Talk to your friends in a normal voice, don't shout. If you yell or run around and the driver has to look away from the road to discipline you, your life could be in danger.

Keep your feet out of the aisle so you won't trip anyone. Don't throw gum wrappers or food on the floor or out of the windows. Even if your mother drives by, don't lean out or wave your arm out the window. You might get hurt if you do.

BICYCLE MANNERS

If you ride your bicycle to school, follow the National Safety Council's rules of the road so that you'll have a safe trip.

Have your bike inspected regularly to make sure it is in

good mechanical condition. Obey all traffic signs, signals and markings, and local ordinances pertaining to bicycles.

Bike on the right side of the road, single file, with the traffic, not against it. Use hand signals to indicate turning or stopping. Be extra careful at all intersections, especially when making a left turn. Look out for drain gates, soft shoulders and other road surface hazards. Watch for open car doors and cars pulling out into traffic.

Don't carry packages or passengers that interfere with your vision or control of your bike. Never hitch a ride on a truck or any other vehicle.

If it's dark in the morning or after school, protect yourself by equipping your bike with reflectors and lights so motorists can see you.

IN CLASS

In some rooms you may be allowed to walk around, talk to classmates, and work on committee projects. Speak softly so you won't disturb others.

If you have an independent assignment, read it carefully and follow directions. When you finish, get another assignment, read a book, or write a story, but keep profitably busy.

Your Teachers

Give your teachers the same respect you give your parents. At home your parents make the rules. Your principal and teachers make the rules at school.

Perhaps you didn't want Mr. Jones as your teacher because you heard that he makes you work hard and gives a lot of homework. But you were assigned to his room and you may as well make the best of it. You'll probably find that Mr. Jones is not so bad after all, and you'll learn a lot in his class.

Don't blame poor grades on your teacher. Ask yourself if you've tried your best and how you can do better. Maybe with a little extra help you'll improve.

Homework

Hand in homework on time. Neat papers in your best handwriting show your teacher that you're trying to do good work.

Classroom Discussion

During a discussion, raise your hand if you want the teacher to call on you. When it's your turn to talk, don't hog the time;

give others a chance, too. It's bad manners to interrupt when someone else is talking. Be a good listener instead. Look at the person who is talking, and think about what he or she is saying.

IN THE CORRIDORS

Never run in the school corridors, even if you're going to recess. Running can cause accidents.

Fire Drills
If there is a fire drill, line up and follow directions for leaving the building safely. The most important thing to remember is not to talk, so you can hear the directions of the person in charge. Obey the directions and keep calm. These rules can save your life if there is an emergency.

The Drinking Fountain
Take your turn, but don't play at the fountain. The next person is thirsty, too. If nobody is waiting behind you, be sure to turn off the water. Don't spit your gum into the fountain. Wrap your gum in paper, and then put it into a waste container.

IN THE LUNCHROOM

Whether you bring your lunch or buy it at school, there are important rules of etiquette for the lunchroom.

Just because one or two people shout and throw food, don't think that's the proper way to act in a school lunchroom. It's not. *You should use the same table manners you were taught at home.* If food accidentally spills on the floor, wipe or pick it up. Someone might slip on it if you don't. Broken glass can cause accidents too.

If you buy your lunch, check the menu in advance so that when you're in line you can order your food quickly. Don't keep the next person waiting while you decide between the peanut-butter sandwich and the taco. Lunch periods are short. Take your seat as quickly as possible. If you can't sit with your friend Stacey, it's not the end of the world. You'll see her later on in the playground.

When you finish eating, throw your garbage into the waste container and leave a clean place for the next lunch group.

IN THE LIBRARY AND MEDIA CENTER

There is usually a lot going on in the library and media center. Speak softly and show concern for others who are working and need to concentrate.

Interrupting and Paying Fines
Don't interrupt the director if there is a class in progress. Come back later. Wait your turn if others are in line ahead of you. If you have to leave, don't throw your library fine on the desk and go. How will anyone know you've paid? Always wait until your payment is recorded.

Care of Books
Take care of the books you use. They are only borrowed from the library and should be returned in the same good condition. Don't write in books, rip them, or break the bindings. Report all damage to the director immediately. Don't

shelve books if you don't know where they belong. Encyclopedias, especially, must be put back in alphabetical order so others can locate the ones they need.

Cassettes and Recorders
If your media center has cassette recorders for independent work in English, math, or languages, don't shove the cassette (audio) in hard. If you don't know how to care for the materials, ask for help. Turn off the cassette recorders and filmstrip viewers when you're finished. Put the learning materials back where you got them. Ask someone to help you if you don't know where they belong.

Use special care when you work with filmstrips. They are costly to replace.

Computers
The computer's monitor and keyboard are not toys to be played with. They are very expensive learning materials. Handle them gently. At most media centers the computer power button is always on. Don't touch it. When you've finished your work, turn off the monitor but not the power.

AT A NEW SCHOOL

Perhaps you and your family have moved to a new city and you are at a new school. How can you make friends and feel that you belong?

How to Make Friends
Start a conversation with the person next to you after class. Say something complimentary. "That's a pretty blouse. Red is a good color for you." Then ask about after-school activities. You can join Scouts, sports, drama, band, or creative

writing classes and meet others with similar interests. Another way to get acquainted is to volunteer to work on a project with a committee.

Lying
Don't brag or exaggerate, and above all don't tell lies. Lying is a bad habit. People lie to show off and to feel important. But it's a cheap way to feel important. Instead, develop your self-confidence by doing your best in school subjects and in after-school activities. You'll feel good about yourself, and it's a better way to win your new classmates' approval and appreciation. You won't have to lie to make an impression. If you lie, your classmates will find you out, and after a while, they won't believe anything you say. Wouldn't *you* rather have friends whose word you can depend on?

Don't lie to escape punishment or sidestep responsibility. It's better to admit what you did and take the consequences than to have it on your conscience. Talk to the person in charge and admit you lied. The punishment will probably be lighter than you thought because you told the truth.

Getting Along with
People Who Are Different
At your new school there may be students or teachers whose skin color or religion is different from yours. Get to know them as individuals before you judge their intelligence or personality. We all want to be thought of as "special," but sometimes we don't give others the same consideration—the right to be different.

Everybody needs friends and wants to feel safe. Belonging to a group makes you feel safe. You know what to expect and what's expected of you when you're with those who are exactly like you. Some people show prejudice by fighting with or separating themselves from those who are different because they are afraid of the unknown. But differences make life interesting.

Get to know others who are different from you. Learn more about them through reading. Novels and works by representative authors can help you understand the customs, traditions, and beliefs of America's many religious groups. The life stories of famous people who have experienced prejudice tell how it feels to be an outsider. Speak out against prejudiced remarks and attitudes. New people can be exciting friends if you use good manners and show them consideration.

When You Meet a New Student
Suppose there is a new girl in your class. When you're eating lunch with your friends you see her eating alone. You know how lonely she feels because you've been through it.

Say "Hi," and introduce yourself. She'll answer and tell you her name. Ask her to sit with you and introduce her to your friends. Start a conversation by asking her questions. "Are you in Scouting?" "Do you like music?" Don't ask embarrassing questions such as, "Why do you wear braces on your teeth?" She is probably very conscious of her braces and it might embarrass her to talk about it. Invite the new girl to your home one day after school.

HANDICAPPED CLASSMATES

Be considerate of your handicapped classmates. Give them a helping hand if they need one, but don't pity them or draw attention to their leg braces, crutches, or wheelchairs. Treat them as you would any other friend.

Talking to a Blind Person
Talk to a blind classmate in your normal voice. Say the person's name to gain his or her attention. Tell a blind person who you are. Say, "Hi, Gerold, this is Marni." When you hand him something, say, "Gerold, this is your book," or "Here's the straw for your malted, Gerold." After Gerold gets to know you, he'll recognize your voice.

Talking to a Deaf Person
Talk slowly and clearly to a deaf person, in a quiet place. Stand where it's well lit and the person can see your face. Turn your head toward him or her when you're talking.

Deaf people use sign language or read lips to "hear" you. Sign language is a real language. Whatever method the deaf use, they can decipher a normal tone better than a shout. If the person has a hearing aid, loud voices will distort the sound.

Slow Learners
Slow learners or retarded classmates like to be included in your games at recess. Make it a simple game of tag or ball, so they can keep up with you. Praise them. Say, "You're doing fine, Mary." Mary will be happy to be able to do something that you do, and you'll be learning a lot: understanding, patience, and caring.

DISHONESTY

Cheating
The dictionary defines cheating as something people do to bring *profit* to themselves. But you often *lose* when you cheat. For example, if you copy your friend Blaine's math

homework, you've lost the opportunity to figure out the problems for yourself. And you probably won't know how to do them on the math test. Also, Blaine spent his time doing the work while you loafed. He won't want to give you his work next time. Cheating can make you lose a friend.

If your teacher sees you cheating on an exam, your paper will probably be thrown into the wastebasket. Even if you knew most of the answers, you won't get any credit. You should have answered the questions you knew and let the others go. Every test grade can't be perfect. It's better to get a lesser grade than to have someone lose their trust in you.

Stealing
If you take something that doesn't belong to you, whether it's a ten dollar bill or a small paper clip, it's stealing. When you steal, it shows you have no consideration for other people's property or their feelings, and no respect for order and parental or school authority.

Some people steal not because they lack the money to buy what they want, but because they must have whatever their hearts desire instantly—without waiting.

At one school, a boy stole objects out of lockers and gave the stolen articles to other boys. He thought they would like him better—play with him or walk to school with him if he gave them presents. His plan backfired and the principal made him return the stolen articles. From then on, none of his classmates wanted to be his friend, especially those he had stolen from. He found out the hard way that stealing wasn't the answer to his problem. It only gave him more problems.

If you feel rejected or disliked, don't give up hope of being liked or loved by turning to destructive behavior like stealing. Talk to a parent, a counselor at school, or a physician. They'll give you sympathy, understanding, and probably some good advice.

Using your best manners at school with your classmates and teachers will help you get along better. A considerate person makes life more enjoyable for everyone.

3 WHEN YOU ARE OUT IN PUBLIC

At home and at school your behavior is judged by your family and friends. When you're out in public, you will be judged by strangers. People you don't know deserve the same consideration you give to those close to you.

Your parents will probably take you to stores, movies, restaurants, and other public places. They will tell you what's expected of you and how to behave. When you're out in public without your parents, always show respect for the person in charge, whether it's a police officer, person of the clergy, bus driver, or a theater manager.

GENERAL RULES AND CUSTOMS

Here are a few important rules and customs to follow when you're on you own out in public.

When you see someone who may need help crossing the street, ask if you can be of assistance. If the answer is yes, put your hand under his or her elbow or offer your arm, and walk slowly. Don't cross until you see the green light or Walk sign.

Watch where you're going when you're on a skateboard or riding your bicycle so that you won't run into others.

Never throw snowballs at passing cars or at unsuspecting people. You could cause a serious accident.

Walk your dog on a leash and respect private property. Be a good citizen and obey signs such as Quiet Zone, near hospitals, and Keep Off the Grass.

SHOPPING TRIPS

When you go to a shopping center, if you accidentally step on someone's toe or bump into another person, say "I'm sorry" or "Please excuse me."

Hold the door open for people coming behind you. It's impolite to let it slam in their faces.

When you're in a store, don't dig around in the packages to find what you want. The entire display may topple. Ask for help from the salesperson or the store manager. Never open a package to see what's in it and then put it back on the shelf. The contents may spill and be wasted. And who wants to buy an opened carton?

If somebody near you drops something, even if he or she is a stranger, help pick it up.

Wait your turn in the checkout line, but if the man behind you has only one or two items and you have many, let him get in front of you. It's the polite thing to do. Have your money ready so you won't have to search your pockets and take up a lot of time.

In an elevator, push the Open button to keep the door from closing until everyone is in.

If you're using a public telephone and someone is waiting, finish your conversation as soon as possible. The person who is waiting may have an important call to make.

ON PUBLIC TRANSPORTATION

Don't be rowdy on the bus or train. "Public" means it's for all the people. If you and your friends play the radio loudly or shout and carry on in a boisterous manner you'll offend others. They have a right to a quiet ride.

Whether you are a boy or a girl, if the bus or train is crowded, give your seat to someone who needs it: a handicapped person, an older man or woman, a pregnant woman, or a person carrying a young child.

If you sneeze or cough on a crowded train or bus, do it into a handkerchief. Turn your face away from the people near you, and say "Excuse me" afterward. Leave the vehicle as clean as you found it.

AT THE MOVIES

Be considerate of other people, especially if you go to the movies with a group of friends. Others paid to see the show, too, and loud, disruptive behavior will keep them from seeing and hearing the actors on the screen.

Proper Behavior
Buy your popcorn when you come into the lobby. Then go inside, find a seat, and sit down. If you're asked, be polite and move over to allow two friends to sit together. Do it even if you aren't asked.

Once the movie starts, don't leave your seat unless it's

important. If you must get up, say "Excuse me" as you go by others who are seated. When you return, say "Thank you, sorry to bother you." If you are the one who's seated and others pass in front of you, stand up and let them go by.

Here are some "don'ts" for moviegoers:

1. Don't run in the aisles.
2. Don't crack gum or stick it under the seat. Wrap it in paper and throw it in the lobby waste container.
3. Don't put your feet up on the seat in front of you.
4. Don't wear a cowboy hat in a movie. Others won't be able to see over you.
5. Don't bring cans of soda into the movie. Cans on the floor can be dangerous.
6. Don't write on the walls or mess up the bathrooms.
7. Don't talk during the movie. But if you must do so, speak softly.

CONCERT AND THEATER PRODUCTIONS

Rules of behavior when going to see live productions are much the same as for attending movies, except that you applaud the performers.

At a concert, you clap when the orchestra leader comes out and bows. Then you applaud at the end of each selection. Sometimes there are silences, but they indicate only the ends of parts of the selection and it's not customary to applaud then. If you're unfamiliar with the music, don't clap until others around you do.

When you're attending a play, it's customary to applaud at the end of each act or scene. People also show approval during a scene when they are especially pleased with an actor's performance by applauding when the actor exits. Singers, dancers, and pop musicians are applauded for specialty numbers during a performance. The more applause performers get, the more they enjoy working for you.

ON SOLEMN OCCASIONS

There are many solemn occasions in life when knowing the right thing to do will make you more comfortable.

At a Church or Synagogue
Be sure to arrive on time for a religious service. If you're late, you'll disturb other worshipers. Boys take their hats off when they enter a church, but in a synagogue it is the custom for men to keep their heads covered. When praying, people are in a meditative frame of mind. Sit quietly. Show respect for others by listening attentively to the service and taking part in it. It's improper to chew gum or to eat during a service in a house of worship.

At a Funeral
Suppose Mr. Jackson, a good family friend, has died. He's someone you were fond of, and you and your parents have decided that you should go to his funeral and pay your respects to his family. Perhaps it's your first experience with death, and you don't know how to behave.

The most important thing to remember is to walk and talk quietly. Dress in neat, clean clothes, and have a respectful attitude for this solemn occasion.

Your parents will write their names and yours in the register, a book for visitors to sign. Walk with your parents to where Mr. Jackson's widow is sitting, and kiss her or shake hands. Say something like "I'm very sorry," or "My deepest sympathy."

Shake hands with Mr. Jackson's close relatives. If the casket is open, you might want to say a prayer or a final good-bye to your friend. If you'd rather not, you can take your seat with the other mourners.

At a cemetery, stand quietly for the final prayer usually said by a person of the clergy.

EATING OUT

Use the table manners you've learned at home when eating at a restaurant. For your early excursions, you can depend on your parents to point the way.

At a Restaurant
with Your Parents
Let's say your family is having dinner at a restaurant. A hostess or headwaiter will greet you and show you to your table. Traditionally, a waiter holds the chairs for the women, and the men will be seated after the women are settled.

Each person will be given a menu. If the menu has foreign words that you don't understand, it's perfectly proper for your parent to ask the waiter to describe the food. Then your parent will help you order.

It's impolite to listen to conversations at other tables or to watch your neighbors eat while you are waiting to be served. Instead, start a conversation at your table and talk quietly.

Don't whistle, or snap your fingers to call a waiter. Ask your parent to tell the nearest waiter to send your waiter to the table.

If the silver or china is dirty, never wipe it off and use it. Tell your parent to ask the waiter for a clean place setting. Should your fork or spoon accidentally fall to the floor, don't pick it up. Your parent will tell the waiter to bring you another.

When the food comes, if it doesn't taste right or it isn't what you ordered, ask your parent to tell the waiter. He'll take the food back to the kitchen and bring you something else.

*Eating at a Restaurant
with Friends*
Perhaps you have permission to have lunch or a snack with friends at a shopping-mall restaurant. You've never been to a restaurant without a parent before, but there's nothing to worry about. Just use the same good manners you used at the restaurant with your family.

Tell the waiter politely, "I'll have a peanut-butter sandwich on whole wheat bread and a glass of apple juice, please." Don't play with the straws or slurp the juice when you get to the bottom of the glass. When the waiter asks, "Will there be anything else?" say, "No, thank you. May I have the check, please?"

If the check says "Please pay the cashier," stop at the desk and pay the check. Otherwise, give the money to the waiter. It's customary at most restaurants to leave a tip on the table for the waiter. It's usually 15 percent of the total bill.

AT A SPORTING EVENT

Whether it's baseball, hockey, soccer, or tennis, all games are based on custom and rules. Manners mean playing by the rules so the game is fair for everyone.

When You Are a Player
Whether you win or lose, don't argue the decisions of those in charge. They won't change their minds anyway, and you'll look like a poor sport. Do your best to win, and if you do, don't brag and hurt the losers' feelings. Try to convince the other team that it was a good match. Say, "You played a good game. We had to fight hard to win."

Never cheat when you're playing a game. If you're losing, fight harder—don't give up until the last point is won. Never quit a game because you're playing badly. If you lose, excuses like "Is the referee your father? He sure gave your team all the breaks" sound like sour grapes. Be a good loser and congratulate the winner.

Don't try to make all the points. Give the other players on your team a chance to score, too. And don't criticize your teammates for making errors. Everyone makes mistakes.

When You're a Spectator
When you go to see a baseball, football, hockey, or soccer game, you can shout for your team at the top of your lungs. But when you're watching games like golf, tennis, or bowling, you must keep quiet until the players have made their shot or point or have taken their turn.

Some fans think it's fun to razz a player, but it's bad sportsmanship. All team members try their best to win. If you were playing the game, you wouldn't like people to boo you, would you?

IN PUBLIC PLACES

Public places, such as the zoo, beach, park, or forest preserve, belong to everyone. Manners in these places are often a matter of your safety. It's your duty to obey the rules.

The Zoo

When you visit the zoo, remember that the animals' cages are their houses and beds, and you are a guest in their homes. You wouldn't throw garbage into a person's home, so don't do it at the zoo. Never feed the animals your leftover lunch, either. All the animals are on a special scientific diet and other foods may make them sick.

Don't ride your bicycle, roller-skate, or use a skateboard at the zoo. You may hurt other visitors or scare the animals. Loud noises will also upset the animals. So will your pet dog or cat. Even a tiny kitten can scare an antelope.

Walk to the exhibits and quietly wait your turn to get inside. For your own safety, don't put your hands into the wild animals' cages. Wild animals might bite, spit, or chew and hurt you. (For example, the spittle of some reptiles can be fatal to humans.)

At the Park or Forest Preserve

Consideration for the environment and for other people are the two basic rules for good manners in the park or forest preserve. These rules are necessary so that we can all enjoy our beautiful natural areas. Don't destroy the places that give you so much pleasure. Help preserve them for future generations.

Ride your bicycle, jog, or hike along the paths. Follow the rules of your sport. You have a responsibility toward others as well as yourself whether you go snowmobiling, fishing, horseback riding, or engage in any other sport.

Be a good camper. Don't litter—use the waste containers. Carelessness with campfires leads to forest fires that kill trees, vegetation, and animals.

Snowmobiles should be ridden only in designated areas, so that precious forests won't be ruined and fish under the ice in streams and small lakes won't be disturbed.

For fishing, buy a license and obey the quota rules. If you catch more fish than the legal limit, throw the extra fish back.

When riding a horse, stay on the bridle paths so that you won't trample the wildflowers and saplings. Use the walk, trot, and canter gaits. Don't gallop around turns. Walk your horse when you meet someone on foot or on horseback coming from the opposite direction.

If you're hiking and see a rider approaching, walk single file. Don't fling sticks or fishing poles in the air, or hit a horse on the rump. It can cause a serious accident. With the rider's permission, pet a horse on the nose. Move quietly; don't come up from behind. You may startle the animal, and it could kick or step on your foot. It's not a pleasant experience when a horse steps on your foot.

On the Beach

When you walk near people lying down at the beach, be careful not to kick sand in their faces. Running, screaming, or ball-playing bothers other beachgoers too.

Don't swim in the ocean without a lifeguard present. There may be Portugese men-of-war or deadly sharks in the water. The lifeguard warns bathers with signals or flags or tells them to keep out of the danger area. He or she also orders everyone out of the water in a thunderstorm because lightning is attracted to water. Always obey the lifeguard promptly.

Even if you think it's fun to push your little brother under the water, don't do it. His lungs may fill with water, and he could panic and drown.

Never pretend you're drowning. If the lifeguard leaves his or her post to rescue you, someone who really needs help may drown. Don't hang around the lifeguard's station. Lifeguards need to give their full attention to the swimmers and the water.

If you're floating on a rubber raft, watch where you're going. The raft is like a surfboard and can injure a swimmer. It can also float out too far from shore.

Use radio earphones so you won't disturb anyone who wants to sleep or read instead of listening to rock music or the ball game.

Littering at the beach is unforgivable. Look around when you're going home. Don't leave anything behind. If you've made a fire, throw water on the coals or embers until the fire's really out. Covering coals with sand isn't enough. People walk barefoot on the beach and can get badly burned if they step on hot coals.

Park pools are fun but they can be dangerous too. Read the rules posted near the pool. Don't swim in the diving area. Don't dive in the shallow water. No running on the pool deck; it's slippery and you may fall. If you have long hair, wear a cap. Place trash, especially bottles, in waste containers near the pool. Shower before entering the pool. Never swim alone or without an adult nearby. Playing ball around a pool is not safe. You may fall and hurt yourself on the concrete or tile.

Showing consideration for strangers when you're out in public is a mark of good manners. It's often a matter of your own safety and well-being too.

4 WHEN YOU ARE AT A PARTY

Whether a party is a small get-together or a large celebration of a special occasion, it should be fun for the host or hostess as well as for the guests.

IF YOU ARE THE HOST OR HOSTESS

Every successful party, whether it is large or small, takes planning. If you want to have a party, the first step is to get your parents' permission. Pick a date that is convenient for them to be there (a parent should always be present), and ask them how many friends you may invite. Then make a guest list. Decide with your parents on some party rules beforehand. Rules may include (1) no food in the living room, (2) no feet on the furniture, and (3) the refrigerator is out-of-bounds for guests.

Giving a Small Informal Party
If you are having a small party for a few friends, don't talk about it at school. You might hurt the feelings of the classmates you didn't invite. Nobody likes to be left out.

Phone your invitations. Tell your guests to dress casually and find out if they can come. Keep the refreshments simple: juice, popcorn, peanuts, raisins, sunflower seeds, and fresh fruit. A nice idea is to prepare a peanut-butter dip. Cut up celery, carrots, zucchini, and cucumbers, and dip the vegetables in the peanut butter. It's delicious and nutritious.

Since your guests already know each other, you needn't worry about introductions and conversations. Be sure everyone is included in the fun, keep the noise level down, and watch that you don't run out of snacks.

Giving a Larger Party
Suppose it's your birthday and you have permission to give a big party. You're going to invite your cousin Allison, your friends at school, and several other boys and girls from summer camp. Invite the new girl in your class; it will mean a lot to her.

Your guests may be invited by telephone or you may send written invitations. A written invitation will help them remember the date and time of the party. But don't send your invitations too early. Ten days before the party is about right. If you are creative, make your own invitations with construction paper and felt-tip pens. If you don't want to make invitations, buy them at the stationery store. Include the following on your invitation:
 1. The occasion
 2. The date
 3. The time
 4. The place if it's not your home
 5. Your name
 6. Your address
 7. Your telephone number
 8. Kind of dress: casual, dress-up, or costume

This is a sample invitation:

> **IT'S A BIRTHDAY PARTY!**
> On Saturday, March 18
> From noon-3 pm Lunch
> Name: Marni Brown
> Address: 3333
>   Greenbriar
> Telephone: 945-4005
> Dress: Casual
>   R.S.V.P.
>   PLEASE COME!

  R.S.V.P. means that the people you've invited should let you know whether or not they are coming to the party. To save time on the telephone, some hosts and hostesses write Regrets Only instead of R.S.V.P. on their invitations. This means that the guests should call only if they can't come. Regrets Only is not always a good idea. The invitation might get lost in the mail, and the person giving the party would wrongly assume that a guest was coming because no call was received.

If one of your guests can't come to your party, have ready the name of another person to invite. But don't tell that person that he or she is second choice. You don't want to hurt anyone's feelings.

Planning the Party
A few days before the party, choose the menu with your parent. Since you are serving lunch, it will involve more food than a small, informal party. A buffet lunch where the guests help themselves to the food is the easiest. One idea is to have a make-your-own-pizza party.

On the buffet table, put out English muffins or pita bread with platters of sausage, cheese, mushrooms, onions, green peppers, tomato sauce, and spices and herbs, such as oregano. After each guest selects the fixings for his or her pizza, place the pizzas on a cookie sheet and pop them into the oven.

Or you might serve tacos. Buy taco shells and put a spoonful of precooked ground beef flavored with taco seasoning mix into each shell. Place shredded lettuce, shredded cheddar cheese, chopped tomatoes, chopped green peppers, sliced pickles, pitted olives, and shredded onions in separate containers. Your guests will select their own toppings.

With either of the above menus, serve cranberry, orange, and apple juice or soft drinks, and peanuts and birthday cake.

Set the buffet table beforehand. Place all the plates, silver, and napkins on the main table. Seat your guests at smaller tables in groups of six or eight. Make place cards so that each person will be seated next to someone he or she knows and nobody will be eating alone.

The Day of the Party
On the day of the party, get dressed fifteen minutes early. Answer the door and say "hello" when your guests arrive. Introduce new friends to your parents. Say, "Mother and Dad, this is Jennifer Peterson. She just moved here. Jennifer, meet my parents."

Tell your guests where to put their coats. Don't look for birthday presents. One of your guests may have forgotten to bring a gift, and it will make him feel uncomfortable.

You don't need a lot of rules for introducing one friend to another friend. Make it simple: "Cristi Barnett, this is Stacey Brown" or even simpler, "Cristi Barnett, Stacey Brown." With two young people of the same age, it doesn't matter whose name comes first. You may want to use a few words of identification to put your guests at ease and give them something to talk about. "Cristi Barnett, this is Derek Kaufman; he's on our park soccer team. Derek, Cristi plays soccer at after-school sports."

If your cousin Allison is carrying a gift, don't rip it out of her hands; wait until she gives it to you. Then say "Thank you." Put it with the other presents and open them all later. Since Allison goes to another school and doesn't know any of your friends, introduce her by saying "This is my cousin Allison Ilene, everybody." Then don't leave her standing alone. Take her over to meet Stacey and say something to start a conversation between them. "Allison, this is my friend Stacey Brown. She's in my homeroom and she loves peanut butter almost as much as you do." Maybe they'll talk about their favorite peanut-butter combinations.

Serving Lunch
When it's time to eat, each guest will take a plate and fill it. Then they will find their place cards and sit at that table.

When all your guests are seated, you may take your turn at the buffet.

You placed Allison on the outside left-hand place next to you because she's left-handed. This will make it easier for her to eat, and she won't be banging elbows with anyone. Stacey is on your other side. Give Allison a little extra attention if she is shy with your friends.

Playing the Games
Let your guests take their turns at the games before you do. If you win, don't accept a prize even if you bought great prizes and would love to have one. You planned the games for your guests' entertainment, and the person who won second place should get your prize.

Opening the Gifts
When you open the gifts, pick the package closest to you and open it. Tell who it is from and show it to everyone. Say something complimentary. "Thanks for the book, Cristi. I really like these mysteries"

Maybe you hate the yellow T-shirt that Derek gave you. But don't hurt his feelings by saying "This T-shirt is yucky!" And don't groan if you receive two or three more T-shirts. Act as if you're happy to see each one, and thank the givers.

It's not good manners to tell Stacey in front of the other guests, "I like your present best of all." The others will be hurt that you didn't like their gifts as much as Stacey's.

Because Allison is your cousin, her present might be more expensive than the others. When you open it don't say "This must have cost your folks a bundle." It's not polite to comment on the price of a gift or to ask what it cost. When you receive a gift, it's the thought—not the price—that counts.

When Your Guests Leave
If your party is still in progress and Cristi has to go home, don't yell from another room, "Bye, Cristi! See ya around!" Leave your other guests for a moment, and walk Cristi to the door. Thank her again for her gift and say, "I'm glad you came to my party."

When the party is over, stand at the door and say goodbye to each guest. After everyone has gone home, thank your parents for the party. Then pitch in and help clean up.

IF YOU ARE A GUEST

Always answer an invitation as promptly as possible. Ask your parent's permission, and tell your host or hostess whether or not you can come. Be definite: "Yes, thank you. I'd love to come to your party." If you must refuse, say, "No, I'm going to visit my cousin Allison on Saturday. But thanks anyway. Hope you have a great party." Don't say, "I'll let you know," and keep that person waiting for your answer. He or she may want to invite someone else in your place.

If you accept an invitation, it's bad manners to cancel because a better invitation comes along later.

Selecting a Gift
If you're invited to a birthday party, always bring a present. Ask your parents to help you shop for it, and spend about what your friends spend on birthday presents. Don't talk about the cost when you give the gift.

Party Manners for a Guest
Review your party manners before you leave home. When you arrive at the party, say hello first to the parents, and

shake hands. Then greet your host or hostess and offer your gift.

When you're introduced to a new person say "Hi" or "Hello," and repeat the name to help you remember it. You might also add, "I'm glad to meet you" or "I've heard a lot about you." Say it only if it's true, though.

Your host or hostess will tell you what games have been planned. Be a good sport and play even if you dislike the games. Complaining will ruin the party. If you win a prize say "Thank you," and don't brag about how good you are. If you lose, don't make excuses.

Never ask, "When do we eat?" Your host or hostess will tell you when it's time to eat. If it's a buffet, don't take more than your share. When the others have had a chance to fill their plates, you may go back for seconds.

If you spill or break something, say you're sorry and clean it up. Then go on with the party. You must try to replace a broken item after the party.

It's not polite to stay longer than the invitation said the party will last. When the party's over, say good-bye to the parents first and thank them. Then say good-bye to your host or hostess. Say, "Your party was lots of fun" or "I had a great time."

A Party with Adults
If you are invited to an adult dinner party where the place settings include more silverware than you use every day, don't panic. Begin to eat with the silver on the outside of the place setting and work your way toward the plate with each course. If you're in doubt, watch your host or hostess or someone else at the table who seems to know what he or she is doing.

There may be more dishes on the table than you're accustomed to. A bread-and-butter plate may be placed on the left above the forks, with a butter knife across the center. A cup and saucer may be placed to the right of the spoons.

At a small party of six or eight guests, wait until everyone is served before you start to eat. At a larger table, after three or four people are served, the host or hostess may say "Please go ahead and eat; the food will get cold." If a cold meal is served, it's polite to wait until everyone is served before you eat.

If you are served unfamiliar foods, such as lobster or artichokes, and you're not sure how to eat them, watch your host or hostess.

The guest who is considerate, appreciative, fits in well, and is fun to be with will be invited back often.

5 WHEN YOU ARE MAKING INTRODUCTIONS

The purpose of introductions is to bring together people who don't know each other. It's all right to be casual when introducing one of your friends to another, but we follow tradition more closely when introducing adults.

TRADITIONAL INTRODUCTIONS

When making introductions involving adults, the custom has always been to say women's and older persons' names first, as well as people with important positions or titles.

Introducing a Man and a Woman
When introducing a man and a woman, it has been customary to say the woman's name first. "Mrs. Peterson, I'd like you to meet Mr. Leonard. Mr. Leonard, this is Mrs. Peterson."

*Introducing an Older Person
and a Younger Person*
When introducing a younger adult to an older person, if you want to show respect, say the older person's name first. Say

HOW DO YOU DO?

"Mrs. Peterson, this is Hal Brown. He's my brother's college roommate. Hal, meet our neighbor, Mrs. Peterson."

Say an adult's name before a child's name. Say, "Mrs. Peterson, this is my friend, Marsha Brown. Marsha, I'd like you to meet Mrs. Peterson, our neighbor."

Introducing People Who Have
Important Positions or Titles
When you introduce a member of your family, it's polite to mention the other person's name first. Say, "Mrs. Vyn, I'd like you to meet my parents. Mom and Dad, this is our library director, Mrs. Vyn." If you and your parents have the same last name, you don't have to mention their name. But if their last names are different from yours, say, "Mrs. Vyn, I'd like you to meet my mother and my stepfather, Mr. and Mrs. Johnson."

To introduce your sister to an important person, say "Superintendent Kahnweiler, this is my sister Betsy. She'll be in the Battle of Books next year. Betsy, Superintendent Kahnweiler gave me my book award."

"Professor Oakley, I'd like you to meet Mr. Wesley. He works with computers, too. Mr. Wesley, this is Professor Oakley."

Introducing People Who Have Special Titles or Degrees

A person who has earned special honors should be introduced by his or her title. People usually let you know how they want to be addressed. We say:

- Doctor Egel, for a person who has the degree of doctor, either medical or academic
- Judge Martay, for a judge
- Father Flanagan, for a priest
- Mr. Milson, for a Protestant minister, or Doctor Milson if he is a doctor of theology
- Rabbi Marx for a rabbi, or Doctor Marx, if he has his doctorate

Forgetting Names

There may be times when you're introducing someone whose name you have forgotten. It happens to all of us. The only thing to do is to say, "I'm sorry, but I forgot your name."

If you're the one being introduced and someone forgets your name, help them out. Say your name quickly. "I'm Joyce, Lori's sister."

Making the correct introductions might seem a bit complicated at first. Just remember the general rule that we honor people who are special by saying their names first. The more you practice introducing people, the easier it will be.

6 WHEN YOU ARE A HOUSE GUEST

Whether you're "sleeping over" at a friend's house for an evening or spending two weeks at your cousin's home, house-guesting is an exciting experience. Use your best manners if you want to be invited back again.

AN OVERNIGHTER

When you're invited to sleep at a friend's home, make sure of the exact time you're expected to arrive and how long you're expected to stay. If you need transportation, arrange for someone in your family to take you there and to pick you up when your visit is over.

Packing
Pack carefully so you won't forget anything and have to borrow from your host or hostess. Your overnight bag should contain pajamas, robe, and slippers; a change of clothing; toothbrush and toothpaste; and a comb and brush. If you take vitamins, be sure to pack them.

Be a Good Guest
Unless you have permission, don't help yourself to food from the refrigerator. If you're hungry or thirsty, ask for something to eat or drink, and do it politely. Say "I'm thirsty, Mrs. Barnett. I'd love a cold glass of milk, please." Mrs. Barnett will give it to you.

Don't be nosy and look in drawers and cabinets or rummage around in your friend's closet just to see what's in it. Those are private areas. Keep out!

Be enthusiastic about the activities that have been planned for you and join in the fun willingly.

Although you'll probably go to sleep later than usual, don't stay up all night talking and laughing or you won't be able to get up in the morning.

When It's Time to Go Home
The next morning, even if your friend begs you to stay, get ready to leave before lunchtime. Pack all your belongings and make sure you haven't forgotten anything. Thank Mr. and Mrs. Barnett for the good time, and when your friend walks to the door with you, say "Thanks a lot. Everything was great!" You might add, "Next time it's your turn to sleep at my house."

A LONGER VISIT

Your mother or father will make arrangements for your two-week stay at your cousin Allison's home. Pack all of the items you took on the overnighter plus several changes of clothing, an extra pair of shoes, a camera (if you have one), and some stationery to write home.

Your aunt will probably give you some empty drawers for your clothes. Unpack your suitcase, and put your things in the drawers. If you live out of your suitcase, your clothes will be a mess.

Allison's Parents' Routine
If your aunt and uncle's routine is different from yours, when you're visiting them, fit into their schedule and obey their house rules. Let's say you like to sleep late on a vacation, but your aunt serves breakfast at eight o'clock. Be at the breakfast table promptly at eight. What if your aunt and uncle sleep late and you're an early riser? Although hunger pains plague you around seven o'clock, you'll just have to wait. Read a book or do some other quiet activity until breakfast is served.

In either situation, don't comment on how different schedules are at your house. The fun of visiting is to see how others live and to learn new ways.

Some Do's and Don'ts
for House Guests
Here are some things guests should and should not do.

- Do make your bed every morning and keep your room neat.
- Do ask your aunt or uncle if you can set the table or help with the dishes.
- Do put books back in the bookcase and records in jackets.
- Do eat what you're served or say "No, thank you."
- Don't spend too much time in the bathroom.
- Don't leave hair or toothpaste in the sink.
- Don't use the telephone without permission; if you call home and it's a toll charge, charge it to your home phone or call collect.
- Don't complain about the food.
- Don't lift pot lids or taste food that is cooking.

Showing Appreciation
Perhaps your aunt and uncle have planned some special activities to make your visit more enjoyable. At the event, you can say, "Thanks, Uncle Sam. This is the best circus I've ever seen." Or, "I've been wanting to see this movie for a long time, Aunt Susy. Thanks for taking me." It shows you appreciate the time, money, and effort they've spent to entertain you.

Going Home
When it's time to leave, take the sheets off your bed and pull the bedspread over the mattress or blankets. Pack everything you brought. Then look under the bed, and check the drawers so you won't leave anything behind.

Before you go, thank your aunt, uncle, and cousin Allison for having you. Thank them even if there were a few boring hours, or if you had a fight with Allison. They tried to show you a good time.

When you get home, write to Allison and her parents before too many days go by, although you thanked them in person. Thank them again for inviting you, and tell them you enjoyed your visit. It's also a generous gesture to send them a thank-you gift. Your parent will shop with you. You might pick a vase because Aunt Susy loves flowers, or a book since Uncle Sam likes to read. Or you can send something good to eat—nuts or fruit. Your cousin Allison will probably like that best. Enclose your letter with the thank-you gift.

Some people would rather bring the gift with them when they go for a long visit. It's perfectly proper to do it that way. But you must still write a thank-you letter when you get home.

WHEN YOU HAVE A HOUSE GUEST

If you've invited your cousin Allison to visit you, tell her the exact time you expect her to arrive and when she is to go home. If the stay is for longer than one night, provide a space in your closet with empty hangers for her. You may also give her a few drawers to put her clothes in.

When Allison arrives, make her feel at home. Offer her something to eat or drink to make her comfortable. Give her a towel, washcloth, a clean glass, and soap. Tell her the house rules. Plan some interesting activities so she'll have a good time.

Whether "guesting" or hosting, the bottom line is respecting other people's feelings and learning to get along together.

7 WHEN YOU ARE WRITING A LETTER

When you become an adult, you'll write business letters as well as letters to friends and relatives. If you practice letter writing now, it won't be a chore when you're older.

THE THANK-YOU LETTER

At your age, you'll probably write more thank-you letters than any other kind. You need to write a thank-you when you receive a birthday or Christmas gift by mail, or get a present for a special occasion such as graduation or confirmation. If you were ill and received a gift, you should write a letter. It's also necessary to send a thank-you after a weekend or longer visit.

It's polite to write a thank-you to your host or hostess after a party saying that you had a good time. But you can telephone a good friend; you don't have to write.

When you are the host or hostess, you might drop a note to thank a guest for a gift, but don't get too carried away or the thank-yous will go on forever. If you're in doubt as to whether or not to write a thank-you letter, it's better to write it.

Write your thank-you letter as soon as possible. If you wait longer than one week to send it, you'll lose some of your enthusiasm, and your writing won't be natural and lively.

Preparing to Write a Thank-You
Don't use a printed thank-you card; it's the lazy person's way. Write your own letter. You don't need fancy stationery or colored ink pens. Use plain white or pale-colored paper and a pen with blue or black ink. Never write in pencil. It rubs off and is hard to read.

Even if you're an excellent typist, don't type your thank-you letter. A letter in your own handwriting makes it personal and special. Leave margins at the top, bottom, and sides. Put the date in the upper right-hand corner. Use your best writing and spelling. Try to be neat and don't cross out too many words. Your letter doesn't have to be long, but it must sound sincere. Tell how you feel, and write the way you talk.

A Thank-You for a Long Visit
This is an idea of the thank-you you might write to Uncle Sam and Aunt Susy for your visit.

Dear Aunt Susy and Uncle Sam,

Thank you for a terrific two weeks at your home! I especially liked the circus. When the clowns came out of that tiny car, I really broke up. You couldn't have picked a better place to take me.

The zoo was great, too. You know how much I love animals. I could have spent days there.

You cooked everything I liked, and it was delicious. I probably gained ten pounds.

Mom and Dad send their best to you and Allison.

          Much love,
          Marni

Besides writing to your aunt and uncle, you should write a separate letter to your cousin Allison.

Dear Allison,
  It was really great spending two weeks with you. Thanks for sharing your room, closet, and drawers. I know I wasn't the neatest. Ha! Ha!
  I liked your friend Blaine. Wasn't his magic show funny? I'm still laughing about the time he tried to pull a scarf from his sleeve and the lining came out.
  I enjoyed playing with your horse collection, too. When you come here, I'll show you some interesting keychains I've collected.
  Hope you can visit me soon.

          Love,
          Marni

A Thank-You for a Gift
Suppose you want to thank your grandmother for her birthday gift. Be sure to mention what the gift was, and tell her why you liked it.

Dear Grandma Mae,
  Thank you for the beautiful sweater you gave me for my birthday. I just love it! It's very special to me

because you made it. I'm going to wear it on the first day of school. I'll think of you every time I put on my lovely blue sweater.

Lots of love,
Marni

Your grandmother will be pleased to know that you've received the gift and that you like it, especially because she spent so much time making it.

Suppose instead of a sweater your grandmother sent you a check. Then you should thank her and tell her what you're going to do with the money.

Dear Grandma Mae,

I really appreciate the generous birthday check. I'm going to use the money to buy new ice skates because I've outgrown mine. We're having skating races in February and I want to do my very best.

I hope you're well and enjoying your exercise class. It sounds like fun.

Thank you so much for never forgetting my birthday.

Loads of love,
Marni

A Thank-You for a Gift
You Didn't Like
Once in a while you may receive a gift you don't like. Perhaps the person who sent it has different tastes from yours. But don't hurt the giver's feelings by saying you don't like the present. Remember, it's not the gift but the thought that counts.

Let's say your mother's friend Rhoda sent you a bracelet for Christmas. You never wear bracelets because they jingle when you practice the piano. But Rhoda spent time and money for your gift, so you must write a thank-you letter whether you like the bracelet or not. Don't lie and say you love the present. Write something like this.

Dear Rhoda,
    Thank you for the bracelet you sent me for Christmas. Inscribing my initial on the clasp gave it a lovely personal touch. It was a very thoughtful gift.

— 78

Our Christmas was beautiful. Aunt Meraly and her family surprised us and came in from Colorado. We had a great time with Debbie and the other girls. Hope you had fun on your holiday too.

With love,
Marni

MORE LETTERS

You may have occasion to write other types of letters. Here are two examples:

Letter of Apology

Dear Mr. and Mrs. Pollara,

I'm very sorry I broke your window. Please have it fixed and send the bill to me. I'm going to pay for it myself by doing errands and baby-sitting.

In the future, instead of playing baseball in our yard, we're going to play in the park.

Sincerely,
Marni Brown

Letter of Sympathy

Dear Agnes,

I was very sorry to receive your letter about your father's death. He was a wonderful person. I'll never forget the way he popped corn and made taffy apples for us the Halloween before you moved away.

My deepest sympathy and love to you and your mother.

Marni Brown

A Longer Letter

When you write a longer letter, number the pages. Put page one on top when you finish. Fold the letter and put it in the envelope with the heading facing the back of the envelope. The person who receives it can take out the letter and read it without having to turn it around.

THE ENVELOPE

Address the envelope with the full names of the people you're writing to. You may put your return address in the upper left-hand corner on the front of the envelope or on the back. The return address can be handwritten or you may use a printed sticker.

There are two forms—block form, where each line begins directly under the last line, or indented form, where each line is set in from the one before.

For your aunt and uncle:

```
Marni Brown
1000 Lincoln Rd.
Lincolnshire, Il. 60015


             Mr. and Mrs. Sam Jones
             3232 S. Eighth St.
             Milwaukee, Wis.
             53215
```

```
Marni Brown
1000 Lincoln Rd.
Lincolnshire, Il. 60015


            Mr. and Mrs. Sam Jones
              3232 S. Eighth St.
               Milwaukee, Wis.
                    53215
```

If your Aunt Susy has kept her maiden name:
   Ms. Susy Smith and Mr. Sam Jones

If your cousin Allison is a pre-teen:
   Allison Jones

If your cousin Allison is a teen:
   Miss Allison Jones
   or
   Ms. Allison Jones

If Allison has a younger brother:
   Master Jeffrey Jones
   or
   Jeffrey Jones

If Allison has a teenage brother
   Mr. Jeffrey Jones

ANSWERING YOUR MAIL

If you receive a letter, don't forget to answer it. The person who wrote is waiting to hear from you. Try to write about things that will interest him or her. Tell what you've been doing, write about people you both know, and ask questions that can be answered in the reply.

These rules of proper etiquette are only a guide to make your life easier and to give you confidence when you face a new situation. People respect those who are mannerly, considerate, and kind. Do your best to make all your relationships pleasant and courteous.

INDEX

Allowances, 17
Apologies, 11, 63, 79
Automobiles, 2

Bank accounts, 17
Beaches, 51, 54
Bicycle safety, 33–34, 52
Borrowing, 17–18
Bus safety, 32–33, 46

Cheating, 41–42, 51
Chores, 11, 17
Compliments, 7, 31
Computers, 38
Curfews, 8

Diaries, 13

Entertainment, 15, 46–47
Etiquette, 1

Families, 3, 10–14
   grandparents in, 13
   siblings in, 12, 13–14
Food, 22–24, 64
   diets, 27
   gum chewing, 31, 36, 47, 48
Forest preserves, 51, 53
Friends, 10, 38–43

Grooming, 27–30
   hairstyles, 29
   oral hygiene, 16, 27–28

Handicapped, 40–41
Hearing aids, 41
Hitchhiking, 34
Hobbies, 15
Homes, 14–15
   bathrooms, 16–17

— 83

Homework, 15
House guests, 68–73

Introductions, 10, 60, 63, 65–67

Letters, 74–82
    privacy and, 13
Libraries, 37–38
Littering, 54–55
Lying, 39

Media centers, 37–38

National Safety Council, 33
Nursing homes, 13

Parents, 6–10, 17, 42
    communication with, 7
    divorce and, 9
Parks, 51, 53, 55
Parties, 56–63
    games at, 61, 63
    invitations to, 57–59, 62
    refreshments, 57
    seating, 59
Peers, 8–9
Pioneers, 2
Post, Emily (*Etiquette, the Blue Book of Social Usage*), 3
Posture, 29
Prejudice, 40
Presents, 60, 61, 62, 72

Privacy, 9, 13–14

Religious services, 48–49
Restaurants, 49–50
    tipping, 50

Schools, 35–40
    after-school activities, 38–39
    class discussion, 35
    fire drills, 36
    homework, 35
Shopping, 45
Sign language, 41
Snowmobiles, 53
Sports, 15, 50–51, 53
Stealing, 42–43
Stepparents, 6, 10
Swearing, 31

Table manners, 18–24, 36–37
Table settings, 19–20, 63
Teachers, 35, 42
Telephone, 2, 13, 24–26, 46
    answering machines, 25–26
    information and unknown callers, 26
Television, 15–16

Women's rights, 3–4

Zoos, 51–52